Gigi & Dar

by Josh Azouz

Gigi & Dar was first presented by Arcola Theatre,
Frenzy Productions, MMXX Productions and
Matthew Schmolle Productions
at Arcola Theatre, London from 3 October 2024.

Gigi & Dar

CAST

SIM	**Roman Asde**
ZOZ/OFFICER REMO	**Chipo Chung**
DAR	**Lola Shalam**
GIGI	**Tanvi Virmani**

CREATIVE TEAM

Director	**Kathryn Hunter**
Designer	**Michael Vale**
Lighting Designer	**Ciarán Cunningham**
Sound Designer	**Jack Baxter**
Movement, Fight & Intimacy Director	**Adi Gortler**
Casting Director	**Helena Palmer** CDG
Assistant Director	**Ralph Jeffreys**
Associate Costume Designer	**Marina Ambrosone**
Production Manager	**Lewis Champney for eStage**
Deputy Stage Manager	**Kayleigh Atkinson**
Assistant Stage Manager	**Amy Moore**
General Manager	**Matthew Schmolle for MSP**

INTERMISSION YOUTH PLACEMENTS

Stage Management	**Helin Sahin**
Lighting Design	**Abi Mensah**

Gigi & Dar was developed with the support of The Bush, The National Theatre, The Royal Court Theatre, Theatre Royal Stratford East and The Yard.

The producers would like to thank Bare Arms for their support with the production.

THE COMPANY

Marina Ambrosone
Marina Ambrosone is an Italian costume designer and maker based in London. Recently graduated in Theatre Costume from RADA, she's interested in developing sustainable costume consumption through vintage and second-hand resources. Some of her recent credits include Associate Costume Designer and Supervisor for *The War of The Roses* (Shakespeare's Globe Youth Company) and Costume Buyer for *Multiple Casualty Incident* (The Yard Theatre).

Kayleigh Atkinson
Theatre credits include: *Message In A Bottle* (US/CAN tour); *Annie Get Your Gun* (Frinton Summer Theatre); *FRAY* (Lilian Baylis); *Long Day's Journey into Night* (Wyndham's Theatre); *Mike Birbiglia: The Old Man and the Pool* (Wyndhams Theatre); *A Little Life* (Savoy Theatre/Harold Pinter Theatre); *Demon Dentist* (UK tour); *Cock* (Ambassadors Theatre); *Abigail's Party* (Park Theatre); *Love, Loss and Chianti* (Riverside Studio); *Groan Ups* (Vaudeville Theatre); *Tales of the Turntable* (Queen Elizabeth Hall); *Pufferfish* (Vault Festival). Kayleigh is thrilled to be involved with *Gigi and Dar*, and excited to be at Arcola Theatre for the first time.

Roman Asde
Roman Asde trained at LAMDA. This is his first professional theatre role.

Josh Azouz
Josh Azouz is an award-winning writer working across stage, screen and radio. His work has been shown in the UK and across the US. Recent plays include: *Kiss/Marry/Push Off Cliff* (NT Connections); *The Get* (BBC Radio 3); *Once Upon A Time In Nazi Occupied Tunisia* (Almeida Theatre); *The Mikvah Project* (Orange Tree Theatre/The Yard Theatre & BBC Radio 4); *Buggy Baby* (The Yard Theatre).
TV includes: *The Night After* (Headlong/BBC 4) and *The Box* (MGM/NENT).
Josh won a Channel 4 playwright award for *Buggy Baby*. The LA Theatre Works production of *Once Upon A Time In Nazi Occupied Tunisia* was nominated for best audio drama at The Audies. Josh has been an associate artist at The Yard Theatre and MUJU (A Muslim-Jewish theatre company).

Jack Baxter
Jack is a sound designer and composer working in theatre and digital media. He trained at the Royal Central School for Speech and Drama.
Theatre credits include: *Grud* (Hampstead Theatre); *The Wolf, The Duck and The Mouse*, *Gulliver's Travels* (Unicorn Theatre); *Between the Lines* (New Diorama); *No Man's Island*, *Redemption* (nominated for sound design Offie) (Big House); *Metamorphoses*, *The Lies You Tell* (New Wolsey); *An Intervention* (Riverside Studios); *Kitchen Sink*, *DNA* (Queen's Theatre Hornchurch); *Not Now, Yes So I Said Yes* (The Finborough); *Our Last First* (The Space); *About 500* (Barbican); *The Lodger* (Coronet); *Cops* (Southwark Playhouse); *Sancho* (Orange Tree Theatre); *The Hunt*, *About 500*, *Albion in Flames*, *Ghosts on a Wire* (Union Theatre).
Film and TV credits include: *Japan Cultural Expo* (Advert), *Mint Chocolate Chip* (Ind.), *The Paddock* (Channel 4), *Wish You Were Here* (Ind.), *This is an Emergency* (Big House), *A Casting Room* (Ind.), *Left* (Ind.), *Traces of Suburbia* (Ind.), *Long Distance Call* (Ind.), *Perils* (RA), *Balance Sheet* (Ind.).
Audio and podcast credits include: *Hustler's Republic*, *I Love Television* and *Moderation* (Bitter Pill Theatre Co.), *Adventures in Pojjland*, *Stuck for Ideas*.

Lewis Champney (Production Manager for eStage)
Theatre credits include: *The Forsyte Saga* (Troupe Productions); *23.5 Hours* (OPM Productions); *The Womens Strike* (Makani); *Captain Amazing* (Matthew Schmolle Productions); *Sorry We Didn't Die At Sea* (The Playwrights Laboratory).
Opera credits include: *Eugene Onegin* (Hampstead Garden Opera)
As Assistant Production Manager: *The Quest, Pandoras Box* (London Youth Opera); *Some Demon, Here* (Papatango); *When It Happens to You*, *The Marilyn Conspiracy*, *Whodunnit 3*, *Kim's Convenience*, *On The Ropes* (Park Theatre); *Dick Whittington*, *Killing Jack* (Queens Theatre Hornchurch); *Playlist for a Revolution*, *Sleepova*, *Paradise Now!* (Bush Theatre); *The Power of Paternal Love* (Barber Institute Opera); *A Single Man* (Troupe Theatre Company).

Chipo Chung
Theatre credits include: *Dido, Queen of Carthage* (RSC); *Julius Caesar* (Sheffield Crucible); *Boys Will Be Boys*

(Headlong); *The Haunting of Hill House*, *The Major of Zalamea*, *Ma Rainey's Black Bottom* (Liverpool Everyman); *Fu Manchu Complex* (Brixton House); *Phaedre*, *The Overwhelming* (National Theatre); *On Religion* (On Theatre); *Turandot* (Hampstead Theatre); *Fallujah* (Truman Brewery/ICA); *Gaudeamus* (Arcola); *Talking to Terrorists* (Out Of Joint); *The Lunatic Queen* (Riverside Studios); *Tall Phoenix* (Belgrade); *Hamlet* (Nuffield Theatre).

Film credits include: *Bladerunner 2049*, *The White Room*, *360*, *In the Loop*, *Sunshine*, *Proof*.

TV credits include: *Silo S1-2*, *Black Cake*, *Electric Eye*, *His Dark Materials*, *Foundation*, *Chimerica*, *Into the Badlands*, *Absentia*, *Moving On*, *From Darkness*, *Thirteen*, *Fortitude*, *Black Mirror*, *The Politician's Husband*, *Sherlock*, *Camelot*, *Casualty*, *Identity*, *Doctor Who*, *The Last Enemy*, *Dalziel & Pascoe*, *Holby City*, *Absolute Power*.

Ciarán Cunningham

Theatre credits include: *Skeleton Crew*, *Silence* (Donmar Warehouse); *Cinderella* (Lyric Hammersmith); *Tambo & Bones* (Theatre Royal Stratford East/ ATC); *Mansfield Park* (Watermill Theatre/tour); *Hey Duggee* – Olivier Award Winner (South Bank Centre/UK tour/Ireland tour); *An Unfinished Man* (The Yard Theatre); *The Sh*t* (Leeds Playhouse/Bush Theatre); *Freedom Project* (Leeds Playhouse); *Me For The World*, *Sound of Yellow* (Young Vic); *Amsterdam* (ATC/Orange Tree/UK tour); *Blood Knot* (Orange Tree Theatre); *One Night In Miami* (Nottingham Playhouse /Bristol Old Vic/Home, Manchester); *Suckerpunch Boom Suite* (Barbican Theatre/Nitrobeat); *Eden* (Hampstead Theatre); *Sleeping Beauty* (Theatre Royal Stratford East); *Shebeen* (Nottingham PlayHouse/Theatre Royal Stratford East); *Last Days Of Iscariot* (Vanbrugh Theatre); *Dublin Carol* (Sherman Theatre); *Into The Woods*, *Brink* (Royal Exchange Theatre); *Wish List* (Royal Exchange Theatre/Royal Court); *Sizwe Banzi Is Dead* (Young Vic/UK tour); *Sense Of Sound's: Migration Music* (Liverpool Everyman Theatre); *Scrappers* (Liverpool Playhouse); *In His Hands; Re:Definition* (Hackney Empire); *Blackout* (The Dukes Theatre); *The Mountaintop* (Welsh National Tour); *When Chaplin Met Gandhi* (Kingsley Hall); *Normal* (Rift); *Chris Dugdale: 2 Face Deception*

(Leicester Square Theatre); *Letter To Larry* (Jermyn Street Theatre).

Adi Gortler

Adi Gortler is a movement director, teacher, and director. She graduated with her MFA in Movement Directing and Teaching from the Royal Central School of Speech and Drama and a B.Ed in Theatre Directing and Teaching from Seminar Ha'Kibbutzim College (Tel Aviv). At the heart of her practice lies a deep celebration of people and their individuality, leading to an environment where uniqueness and identities are cherished and expressed in creating a story.

Her latest work includes: As Movement Director: *Baghdaddy*, *Jews. In Their Own Words* (Royal Court); *The EU Killed My Dad*, *The Anarchist* (Jermyn Street Theatre); *The Snow Queen* (Polka Theatre); *Attempts On Her Life* (Guildhall); *Cyrano De Bergerac*, *Bad Roads*, *Swive*, *How To Hold Your Breath*, *The Antipodes*, *Light Falls*, *Woyzeck*, *Pomona* (LAMDA); *Borders* הגדר ألسياج (Vault Festival/Drayton Arms/OSO Arts Centre).

As Intimacy Director: *The Shape Of Things* (Park Theatre); *Cyrano De Bergerac*, *Bad Roads*, *Swive*, *How To Hold Your Breath* (LAMDA).

As Director: *A Trip To Heaven* (Upstairs at the Gatehouse); *What Moves You?* (LAMDA); *I See in Colour* (International Children's Theatre Festival, Haifa); *As a Matter of Fact – The Post Truth Cabaret* (Habima Theatre, The Arab-Hebrew Theatre, Tzavta, Haifa Theatre).

Kathryn Hunter

Kathryn Hunter is an Olivier Award-winning actor and director. She won Best Supporting Actress at the New York Film Critics Circle Award in 2021 for her role in Joel Coen's *The Tragedy of Macbeth* with recent screen highlights also including *Poor Things* (dir: Yorgos Lanthimos) and films *Megalopolis* (dir: Francis Ford Coppola) and *The Front Room* (dir: Max & Sam Eggers), released in September 2024.

Theatre Directing credits include: *Napoleon Disrobed* (Told by an Idiot/Arcola/Theatre Royal Plymouth); *Out of Blixen* (Print Room), *Othello* (RSC); *The Birds* (National Theatre); *Mr Puntila and his man Matti* (Almeida Theatre/Albery Theatre/Traverse Theatre); *Wiseguy Scapino* (Theatre Clwyd); *The Glory of Living* (Royal Court); *The Comedy of*

Errors, *Pericles* (Shakespeare's Globe); *My Perfect Mind* (Told by an Idiot/Young Vic and tour).

Ralph Jeffreys

Ralph Jeffreys is a young theatre director who has recently graduated from the University of Cambridge. His work as a director includes *Bugles at the Gates of Jalalabad* and *Prairie du Chien* (BATS Theatre); *Summer and Smoke* (ADC Theatre); *Phaedra's Love* (Pembroke Players) and the award-winning play *LOUD* (Corpus Playroom). This is his first professional theatre role.

Amy Moore

Amy Moore started working in theatre as a college summer job in Frinton-on-Sea, moving into stage management after four years of box office and front of house. She has just finished another summer season in Frinton as Company manager.

Recent theatre work includes: *Daivid Copperfield* (Frinton-On-Sea/Riverside Studios); *Spy For Spy* (Riverside Studios).

Recent opera work includes: *The Ringcycle* (Regents Opera)

Helena Palmer CDG

Helena is a freelance casting director with over twenty years' experience.

She began her casting career at the Royal Exchange, Manchester and then with the National Theatre. She was Casting Director at the Royal Shakespeare Company from 2008 to 2021, casting over fifty classical and contemporary plays.

Recent projects include: *An Inspector Calls* (PW Productions – 2024 UK tour); *The Glass Menagerie* (Rose Theatre, Kingston and tour); *Untitled F*ck M*ss S**gon Play* (Manchester Royal Exchange/Young Vic); *No Pay? No Way!*, *Cat on a Hot Tin Roof*, *Beginning* (Manchester Royal Exchange); *The Tempest*, *Cymbeline* (Royal Shakespeare Company); *Linck & Mülhahn*, *Mary*, *The Fever Syndrome* (Hampstead Theatre); *The Dream of a Ridiculous Man*, *The White Factory*, *Dmitry* (Marylebone Theatre); *Miles*, *The Fall*, *Tikkun Olam* (Original Theatre Company); *The Wind in the Willows*, *The Child in the Snow* (Wilton's Music Hall); *Sarah* (Coronet Theatre); *Blackmail*, *Antigone* (Mercury Theatre, Colchester); *The Mirror and the Light* (Gielgud Theatre).

Helena is a member of the Casting Directors' Guild.

Helen Sahin
Helen started her production journey at the beginning of 2024 as an Assistant Stage Manager with Intermission Youth Theatre.

Lola Shalam
Lola Shalam trained at Guildhall. Her credits include *Macbeth* (Wessex Grove/Underbelly/Shakespeare Theatre Company) and *Women, Beware the Devil* (Almeida Theatre).

Abi Mensah
Abi joined Intermission Youth's production trainee programme in Feb 2024, getting lighting and sound design training. Other training includes: LAMDA backstage tour and introduction to technical production and lighting designer for *Romeo and Juliet* on the Intermission Youth Youngers Show, April 2024.

Michael Vale
Michael Vale has designed the sets and costumes for well over two hundred theatre and opera productions both in the UK and abroad including those he has directed. Companies he has worked with include: The Royal Shakespeare Company; The National Theatre; The Royal Opera House; English National Opera; Glyndebourne Festival Opera; Opera North; The Royal Festival Hall, London; De Vlaamse Opera, Antwerp; Los Angeles Opera; New Zealand International Art's Festival; The Ibero-American Theatre Festival in Bogota; Hong Kong Academy for the Performing Arts; Galaxy Theatre, Tokyo; Warsaw Globe Theatre Company; Munich Biennalle; The Black Theatre of Harlem and The Royal Court Theatre, London. His work has received an Olivier Award, an LA Stage Scene Award and has been nominated for three further Olivier Awards.

Tanvi Virmani
Tanvi Virmani trained at Bristol Old Vic Theatre School. Theatre credits include: *Cyrano* (Traverse Theatre); *Minority Report* (Nottingham Playhouse/Birmingham Rep/Lyric Hammersmith); *The Crown Jewels* (Garrick); *Two Billion Beats* (Orange Tree Theatre); *Life of Pi* (Wyndham's/tour); and *The Tempest* (Theatre Royal Bath). TV credits include: *Not Going Out*.

The world premiere production of *Gigi & Dar* was supported by Arts Council England Project Grants.

Since 2018 MSP has independently produced critically acclaimed theatre and performance across mid-scale, studio, festival and fringe, both nationally and internationally.

www.matthewschmnolleproductions.com

MMXX (Twenty Twenty) is an independent, cross-media production house driven by a passion to create meaningful, original content for national and international audiences, with a focus on distinctive, authored content.

Founded by Robert Delamere and Holly Gilliam, in 2020, MMXX brings together their extensive experience across film, TV, live events, theatre, podcasts and talent management.

www.mmxxproductions.com/

The producers would also like to thank Richard Morris, Michaela Rees Jones and Stuart Roden for their support.

YOUTH

For the 2024 Production of *Gigi & Dar*, the producer partnered with Intermission Youth Theatre to create two paid placements for young people during the production period.

Intermission Youth (IY) use theatre and Shakespeare to help transform the lives of young people in London through, theatre, film, and whole person support. Established in 2008, our experience has repeatedly demonstrated that a supportive environment can bring forth young people's creativity and confidence, and build valuable life skills leading to healthy, positive choices and a greater sense of ambition.

www.intermissionyouththeatre.co.uk/

arcola
theatre

Arcola Theatre was founded by Mehmet Ergen and Leyla Nazli in September 2000. Originally located in a former textile factory on Arcola Street in Dalston, in January 2011 the theatre moved to its current location in a former paint-manufacturing workshop on Ashwin Street. In 2021, we opened an additional outdoor performance space just around the corner from the main building: Arcola Outside.

Arcola Theatre produces daring, high-quality theatre in the heart of East London. We commission and premiere exciting, original works alongside rare gems of world drama and bold new productions of classics. We work with creatives from across the globe, acting as a platform for emerging artists, providing them space to grow and explore, and similarly as a refuge for established artists refining their craft. Our socially engaged, international programme champions diversity, challenges the status quo, and stages trailblazing productions for everyone. Ticket prices are some of the most affordable in London, and we offer concessions for under 26s, senior citizens, those on disability benefits and unemployment benefits, as well as industry union members. We produce the yearly Grimeborn Opera Festival, hosting dozens of new and classical works from across the globe.

As part of our commitment to supporting the diversity of the theatre ecosystem, every year, we offer 26 weeks of free rehearsal space to culturally diverse and refugee artists; and our Participation department creates thousands of creative opportunities for the people of Hackney and beyond. Our pioneering environmental initiatives are award-winning and aim to make Arcola the world's first carbon-neutral theatre.

Arcola has won awards including the UK Theatre Award for Promotion of Diversity, The Stage Award for Sustainability and the Peter Brook Empty Space Award.

arcola theatre

Artistic Director Mehmet Ergen
Deputy Artistic Director & Executive Producer Leyla Nazli
Head Of Marketing & Communications Laura Evans
Marketing Manager Monique Walker
Associate Artist & Production Coordinator Katharine Farmer
Production Coordinator Rebecca Hobbis
Operations Managers Catriona Tait and Carmen Keeley Foster
Finance Manager Steve Haygreen
Participation Manager Charlotte Croft
Technical Manager Matthew 'Lux' Swithinbank
Software Developer & IT Support Oliver Brill

Trustees
Andrew Cripps (Chair)
Naz Yeni (Vice Chair)
Ben Todd
Gabriel Gbadamosi
Abdullah Tercanli

With grateful thanks to our Front of House, Technical and Bar teams, as well as all of our Supporters and Volunteers. Finally, thank you to our wonderful cleaner Milton Vargas Rodriguez.

GIGI & DAR

Josh Azouz

Thanks

A special thank you to Kathryn Hunter, and the original cast and creative team.

To the people who have helped develop this play: Shyvonne Ahmmad, Gemma Barnett, Luca Kamleh Chapman, Robert Delamere, Omar Elerian, Pooja Ghai, Holly Gilliam, Georgia Green, Laura Hanna, Daniella Issacs, Dean Judkowsky, Flora Spencer Longhurst, Rory McGregor, Adi Noy, Stewart Pringle, Matthew Schmolle, Giles Smart, Amalia Vitale, Ashleigh Wheeler.

Lastly to Amanda. For everything.

Characters

GIGI, *female, nineteen*
DAR, *female, twenty*
ZOZ, *female, forty*
SIM, *male, sixteen*

OFFICER REMO, *voice-over, female, aged twenty-two*
This character could be voiced live (off-stage) by the actor who plays ZOZ.

Setting

A remote area in a contested land
It begins barren
Later, it flowers
Unless it's just a stage. And all is imagined.

Time

2016, but time misbehaves.

Notes on the Text

An ellipsis … denotes a struggle to clarify a thought, or an unspoken thought.

Words in square brackets [ ] should be played by actor not spoken out loud.

Double space, or more, between lines are invitations for longer silences and / or non-verbal action.

Characters move seamlessly between talking to each other and talking to the audience.

The lyrics from Dar's song are 'Toothpaste Kisses' by The Maccabees. These could be substituted for something else.

This text went to press before the end of rehearsals and so may differ slightly from the play as performed.

Lights up on a barren space.

A chain of spikes might run across the ground.

Upstage is a colourful concrete cabin.

Downstage is a sun umbrella and a couple of brightly coloured canvas chairs.

GIGI *and* DAR *enter.*

GIGI *plants a shovel ominously into the ground.*

DAR *throws down some metal parts.*

GIGI *and* DAR *assemble their M4s.*

After they finish building their guns, they sit on the chairs.

An alarm goes off on DAR*'s watch.*

DAR *turns to the audience.*

DAR. Welcome to roadblock 432.

Now I know what you're thinking. Where are the gun towers? Where are the dogs? Yeah, we don't need that. We've been dropped in deserts without water. We've climbed mountains in our pyjamas. So sit back, relax, make yourself comfortable – it's an eight-hour shift. Hey, don't look so worried, nothing ever happens here – does it G?

GIGI *gives* DAR *a look.*

Okay things happen. But not here. And certainly not to us.

I'm Dar. This is Gigi.

GIGI. Hi.

DAR. Normally Gigi is chatty, can't shut the girl up – Why are you being shy?

GIGI. [I'm not being shy.] Just do the time and place.

DAR. For security reasons we can't tell you where this roadblock is. To be fair we're not too sure ourselves. The borders keep changing. But we're good on time. We're excellent on time. I'm gonna come straight out and tell you the time. No bullshit. Real talk. It's a Sunday. What year?

GIGI. 2016.

DAR. Yeah, nice. We've been in service for 724 days – time gets loopy after 724 days. Did we want to join the army? Would you want to eat a wolf's testicle? We were drafted and 724 days later we're still here. Now, are we crying? Are we fuck. In six days we finish the army! SIX DAYS! And after that, no more white cheese, no more tying our hair up, no more burnt toast ever again. We're gonna travel the world, get high, and dance away our trauma.

GIGI. You're full of yourself today.

DAR. I'm just buzzing – you know why I'm buzzing!?

GIGI. We'll talk about that later.

DAR. I've got big news.

GIGI. Later!

DAR. So after the army we're gonna go travelling. Like not immediately, I'll have to wait tables first. Not Gigi. She's rich.

GIGI. They don't need to know this.

DAR. Her dad is a cabinet minister for the ruling party. Picture a party on the right. Now imagine them a bit further right. A bit further. Little bit further right. And they're all weapons trained.

GIGI. Finished?

DAR. Will your dad pay for your travels?

GIGI. No.

DAR. Will he pay for mine?

GIGI. What?

DAR. I'd kill not to wait tables, to spend six months learning how to think again. I swear my head has actually shrunk.

GIGI. It's bigger than ever.

DAR. Yeow! You're just lucky – you can read, watch films, go to museums, maybe not museums, but you know just return to seeing the world in colour again – I swear I only see in black and white – I'm like an old film!

GIGI. Dad is making me work to get votes.

DAR. Typical! Hey we can work in the same restaurant!

GIGI. It's quite far away.

DAR. You can come stay! The army's brilliant cos you meet all these people you would never normally meet. I'm a straight-A student, part-time DJ and from the capital. Gigi is from the suburbs, she's religious and got eczema. Now we're best friends.

GIGI. Dar.

DAR. I'm just messing, she knows I'm messing. Tell them how we became friends.

GIGI. During basic training, we schemed up all these ways to get days off.

DAR. We drunk cigarette ash, hoping to get a fever.

GIGI. Thought I'm telling them this bit.

DAR. Sorry – I'm hyper!

GIGI. We slept with potatoes and prayed they would absorb the calcium from our bones. We wanted to wake up broken.

   DAR *and* GIGI *strike a pose as if all their bones are broken.*

GIGI. You look like that dog.

DAR. What dog?

GIGI. Up north – broke her leg. You made a splint using a popsicle stick.

DAR. Oh yeah.

GIGI. That was when I thought you were more than just a narcissist.

DAR. Yeow!

GIGI. You know I love you.

DAR. Line up behind the rest.

GIGI. I mean I respect you.

DAR. What are you – the mafia?!

DAR *looks at* GIGI *quizzically for a beat.*

GIGI. Loads of Americans kill themselves!

DAR. What?

GIGI. Like more American soldiers kill themselves than die in combat.

DAR. ...Okay.

GIGI. It's a fact.

DAR. Why are we talking about this?

GIGI. The Americans are thousands of miles from home – they've no clue why they're fighting, but us, our siblings fought, our parents fought, our grandparents fought – we know why we're fighting.

DAR. I hope the party are paying you for this.

GIGI. We're like loyal beyond the grave.

DAR. Have you been fucking your dad?

GIGI. Trust, loyalty, it's in our blood – and service thickens the blood.

DAR. Oh my god you're embarrassing yourself.

GIGI. I'm serious – I would die for you.

DAR. Stop showing off!

GIGI. It's true.

DAR. Then you're a fool.

GIGI. A bad guy comes here now you wouldn't take a bullet for me?

DAR. Probably not.

GIGI. Would you take a bullet for Nas?

DAR. Yes.

GIGI. If it was between Nas and, like, your mum who would you save?

DAR. My mum! No Nas! No Mum! My dad? No definitely Nas.

GIGI *stews on this answer for a beat.*

GIGI. What's the time?

DAR. Er, where's your watch?

GIGI. At home.

DAR. You're lucky Officer Remo didn't notice.

GIGI. She did. I'm cleaning the toilets straight after duty.

DAR. *Bitch.* Hopefully you guys won't meet Officer Remo. Although her vagina smells of freshly cut grass.

GIGI. Ha!

DAR. For real, it's like springtime down there.

GIGI. How could you possibly know that?

DAR. I couldn't sleep one night.

GIGI. SHUT UP.

DAR. What's the big deal?

GIGI. When?!

DAR. In the navy.

GIGI. That was last year! How are you only telling me this now!?

DAR. Why are you being such a homophobe?

GIGI. I'm okay with women.

DAR (*a look to audience*). Course you are.

GIGI. I just don't like the smell of freshly cut grass.

DAR. I can smell yours from here.

GIGI. Stop stop, did you actually go with Officer Remo?

DAR. Like I'd cheat on Nas with Remo.

GIGI. You bastard!

DAR. Ed Sheeran, though.

GIGI. Ed Sheeran now?

DAR. Gingers are so exotic.

GIGI. Last week it was Obama.

DAR. Yeah but he's still really into Michelle. The kids are doing great – I'm not a homewrecker. Are you still on Harry Styles? When we first met Gigi was *obsessed*.

GIGI. Now I'd have any of them.

DAR. The whole of One Direction?

GIGI. Obviously not at the same time.

DAR. Why not?

GIGI. That would be gang-rape.

DAR. Whoa whoa whoa you'd be in control.

GIGI. I'm not sure you'd ever be in control with that many guys.

DAR. Course you would – they're singers – you've got an M4. Oh my god this is good – *this is so good* – so they're here – the whole of One Direction is here –

GIGI. I don't think sex would be on their mind.

DAR. [Why?] I'm beautiful, you've got a hole.

GIGI. Bitch!

DAR. Seriously, how would you manage the fuck party?

GIGI. It's not exactly secluded.

DAR. *But it is remote.* You could have your way, and no one would ever know.

Literally nothing ever happens here. There should be at least four soldiers per roadblock, but cos we're at the end of the world, they just rotate twos.

GIGI. Now they think we're just saying that and something major will happen.

GIGI *and* DAR *take out their binoculars and survey the horizon.*

Pause.

They put their binoculars down.

DAR. Okay so One Direction are here – naked, erect, panting.

GIGI. Firstly they wouldn't all be here together. They're all attempting solo careers, Louis is a dad, it's unlikely they're gonna have time to hang out. And secondly if they were to get back together for a reunion gig, which I obviously pray for every night, they're gonna play major capital cities – not roadblock 432.

DAR. Reality aside.

GIGI. Yeah that's getting harder.

DAR. Huh?

GIGI. It's like hard to, imagine…

DAR. Okayyyyy – One Direction decide to tour the country, and because they're prettier than they are smart they think roadblock 432 is worth a visit, so they get in their limo and head east, and oh look, two gorgeous soldiers are flagging them down.

The limo stops.

They get out.

Private Gigi. One Direction awaits your commands.

GIGI....Liam would sing. I'd get Niall to go down on me. Louis would do me doggy. While I just look at Harry.

Beat.

DAR. What about Zayn?

GIGI. I didn't know we were including Zayn.

DAR. Why wouldn't we include him?

GIGI. Coz he left the band before they split.

DAR. Well Zayn is very much here. Cock like a truncheon. Yet feeling left out.

GIGI. Right. Um... I think I'd marry Zayn.

DAR (*flat*). Wow, okay.

GIGI....Or I just like cover his body in custard, and lick him.

DAR. You hate the idea of blowjobs.

GIGI. I wouldn't lick him down *there*.

DAR. What are you licking then – his knee?

GIGI. I don't know!

DAR. When you're with someone you love, and being married to Zayn I presume you are in love, you may have to do stuff you're not arsed for.

GIGI. I am not doing *that*.

I'll remove a couple of his ribs, he can do it himself.

Pause.

DAR. Last night I dreamt I'd die during this shift.

GIGI. God forbid.

DAR. Now it's going round and around in my head. Like a song stuck on repeat. This go-kart is racing towards me –

GIGI. I don't wanna hear it!

DAR. Well you're fucking gonna! This go-kart is racing towards me. The driver takes out his gun and BAM. I am killed with a shot to the head, but first I get hit in the belly button. Right in the bullseye. It's almost stupid. I go to laugh, but then the head-shot tears off my face.

GIGI. Where am I?

DAR. Not here. I die alone.

GIGI. Well now you've said it out loud it obviously can't happen.

Beat.

DAR. Time game?

GIGI. Yes!

DAR. This is a game where we guess how long left we have of our shift.

GIGI. 334 minutes.

DAR. 370 minutes.

DAR *looks at her watch.*

DAR. 402 minutes.

GIGI. Aii!

DAR. Gigi lost cos my guess was closer to reality. Truth or dare.

GIGI. What?

DAR. You know the rules. Every first round. Truth or dare.

GIGI. Truth.

DAR. Okay – would you –

GIGI. Dare.

DAR. You always choose truth.

GIGI. Well today I'm switching it up. Dare.

Beat.

DAR. Okay, dare.

Fire grenade thirty.

GIGI. Absolutely not.

DAR. You said dare!

GIGI. We haven't got ear-plugs.

DAR. If we go temporarily deaf, time might go faster.

GIGI. What!?

DAR. Shoot me with rubber bullets.

GIGI. Shoot *you*!?

DAR. Last time I shot at you I felt terrible.

GIGI. How does that work then?

DAR. The best thing about the dare is the guilt.

GIGI. Why do you want me to feel guilty!?

DAR. Guilt hangs around a lot longer than a bruise.

GIGI. I'm not gonna shoot you –

DAR. I'll walk sixty metres, no danger –

GIGI. Choose something / else –

DAR. It'll barely make an impact.

GIGI. What about IV bags?

DAR. That's not a dare, that's a vibe!

YEOW! In my bag is a tub of Nutella!

GIGI. Fuck that.

DAR. What is this? You lost the game.

GIGI. I smell the stuff I put on five pounds.

DAR. PRIVATE GIGI GO FETCH THE NUTELLA!

GIGI. PRIVATE DAR IF I GOTTA EAT IT, I'M NOT FETCHING IT!

A face off.

DAR *exits into the cabin.*

GIGI *turns to the audience. Pause.*

GIGI. Last night my cousin had sex with Dar's boyfriend.

Do I tell her?

DAR *enters with a tub of Nutella and hands it to* GIGI.

DAR. There's no spoon.

GIGI *eats the Nutella with her fingers.*

Some time.

Enough.

GIGI *keeps eating.*

GIGI *tosses the tub.*

DAR. You risk your life for the land – and then you litter!?

GIGI *walks away.*

GIGI *takes off her helmet and lets down her long hair.*

DAR. Gigi!?

GIGI. I want to wear it down.

DAR. Put it back on.

GIGI. It feels amazing.

DAR. If a patrol swings by we'll both lose weekends.

GIGI *walks further off.*

DAR. Gigi… I get it…

GIGI. You do?

DAR. I still shower with earrings.

GIGI. You're just saying that.

DAR. I'm not.

And the other week… in the middle of the night… I woke up and put on lipstick.

GIGI (*slight sneer*). Did you feel like a *girl*?

DAR. PRIVATE GIGI PUT ON YOUR HELMET!

GIGI ties up her hair and puts on her helmet.

You're acting weird. What's going on?

Beat.

GIGI. Last night…

I went to the Block.

DAR. The Block Block?

GIGI. Yeah.

DAR. You never go to clubs.

GIGI. Tina invited me.

DAR. Tina? Where was my invite?

GIGI. You didn't finish till midnight.

DAR. I could have come after.

GIGI. Dar don't be like that.

DAR. What did Tina wear?

GIGI. Not much.

DAR. Sounds about right. So?

GIGI. So… I went to the Block and –

DAR. Wait last night – Saturday!? – Nas was at the Block!

GIGI. Yeah. I know.

DAR. Did you see him?

GIGI. For like a minute.

DAR. He look cute?

GIGI. I mean, yeah.

DAR. You don't think Nas is cute?

GIGI. I think he's – yes cute. Anyway so we're in the Block and I see Mump.

DAR. Officer Remo's Mump?

GIGI. Yeah.

DAR. Mump was at the Block?

GIGI. Yes.

DAR. He's very old he must be thirty.

GIGI. Maybe.

DAR. That's nuts. Our officer dates Mump – how to describe Mump? He's a fridge.

GIGI. Why a fridge?

DAR. Square, pale, cold.

GIGI. I think he's sweet, like he's quiet, but he listens really well.

DAR. Everyone thinks quiet people are good listeners. People say that about Nas.

GIGI. Mump is a good listener. And when he actually says stuff, it's profound.

DAR. What did he say?

GIGI. No, nothing, but we were talking –

DAR. How? The bass in that joint is like an earthquake.

GIGI. Outside, we talked, we…

DAR. What…?

GIGI. We…

Smoked.

DAR. You smoked a cigarette, friend?

GIGI. Yeah.

DAR. I've been offering you cigarettes for time.

GIGI. I know.

DAR. Thanks for having all these experiences without me.

GIGI. Sorry.

DAR. So you and Mump?

GIGI. Yeah so we talked, and, and…

DAR. Wait where was Tina during all this?

GIGI. With me!

DAR. And?

GIGI. We made out.

DAR. You and Tina!?

GIGI. No.

DAR. You and Mump?

GIGI. Yeah.

DAR. You and Remo's Mump?!

GIGI. Yes.

DAR. YES, FRIEND! And then?

GIGI. Tina and me left the club.

DAR. That's it??

GIGI. Yes.

DAR. That's a really good story.

GIGI. I'm an awful human being.

DAR. Shutup. Is Mump a good kisser?

GIGI. Very. On the bus back here, I started imagining the life we would have together, where we would live, what side of the bed I'd sleep, how many children.

DAR. Oh my god you need to lay him already!

GIGI. And I was on my phone, stalking him loads, looking at photos from way back, like from his childhood birthdays – am I a paedophile?

DAR. I stalk everybody all the time.

GIGI. I feel really bad.

DAR. You only kissed?

GIGI. Yeah.

DAR. So next time you see him make it super clear you're into him.

GIGI. How?

DAR. 'What-up Mump, let's go to the toilets.'

GIGI. I'll burn in the next world.

DAR. You'll burn in this world if you *don't*.

GIGI. It's wrong, he's with Remo.

DAR. It's *his* wrong, not yours.

GIGI. I can't stop thinking about him.

DAR. YEOW! You've got someone to long for, to miss. Tonight call Mump up, have thirty seconds phone sex, log a couple of images and then you'll be good for an eight-hour shift.

GIGI. I don't wanna long for, I don't wanna miss – aiiii.

DAR. So touch yourself.

GIGI. Won't that make me want him more?

DAR. Nyeh, it'll get him out of your system.

GIGI....

GIGI walks off.

DAR. What are you doing?

GIGI. What does it look like?

DAR. Now!?

GIGI. If the baddies show up, call me.

GIGI exits to the cabin.

DAR looks at us.

DAR. Yo, she's never done that before. This isn't that type of show.

Checks the coast is clear. Takes out her phone and leaves a voice note.

Hey... just to say I miss you... I want to eat your face. Bye.

DAR puts her phone away.

Sound of a patrol car arriving. OFFICER REMO's *voice booms from a megaphone.*

OFFICER REMO (*voice-over*). ATTENTION.

DAR. OFFICER REMOI!

GIGI sprinting out from the cabin.

GIGI. OFFICER REMOI!?

DAR snorts a laugh.

OFFICER REMO (*voice-over*). Why can I see a tub of Nutella on the ground?

DAR. That was me –

OFFICER REMO (*voice-over*). You've been eating Nutella?

GIGI. She's lying!

DAR. Honest, I was hungry.

OFFICER REMO (*voice-over*). You fat fucking bitch!

GIGI. It was me!

OFFICER REMO (*voice-over*). SHUT-THE-FUCK-UP GIGI!

Drop down, both of you.

Twenty.

GIGI *and* DAR *do twenty press-ups.*

Nutella on duty, what is this, a slumber party?

GIGI. No Officer Remo.

DAR. No Officer Remo.

OFFICER REMO (*voice-over*). Who ate the Nutella?

GIGI *and* DAR. I did.

OFFICER REMO (*voice-over*). Private Dar you're already on a warning, and Private Gigi you've got bad skin. WHO ATE THE NUTELLA!?

DAR *laughs.*

Laugh again and it'll be thirty.

DAR *keeps laughing.*

Okay thirty.

DAR *collapses with laughter.*

Forty.

The laughs die.

The girls finish their forty press-ups.

Private Dar you're making me coffee for the rest of the week. I'm also gonna radio every unit in the area to do regular patrols. If they catch you doing anything, I'll speak to Commander Quin about extending your service – CLEAR?

DAR. Yes Officer Remo.   GIGI. Yes Officer Remo.

Beat.

OFFICER REMO (*voice-over*). Mump went to the Block last night. Said he saw you.

GIGI. Did he? I didn't see him, it's a big place, busy place, Officer Remo.

OFFICER REMO (*voice-over*). I thought you were too religious for clubs.

DAR. That slag Tina dragged her along.

OFFICER REMO (*voice-over*). I don't know Tina.

DAR. She's... tall.

OFFICER REMO (*voice-over*). Oh. Tina. Yeah. Slag.

If you need to let off steam, shoot rubbers.

The sound of the patrol car driving off.

GIGI. Bummer about coffee duty.

DAR. It's cool, I'll wash her mug out in the toilet.

So Mump is the reason you been shy?

GIGI. Yeah... stupid.

DAR. Did Tina see Nas?

GIGI. What?

DAR. At the Block did Tina talk to Nas?

GIGI. Like I said, we just saw him on the way out.

DAR. I don't trust Tina.

DAR *stares at* GIGI.

GIGI. 306?

DAR. Overestimate. Then the right time will be less painful.

GIGI. 323?

DAR *checks her watch*.

DAR. 341. Maybe I should smash my watch?

GIGI. What's this now?

DAR. Might be easier to not know the time.

GIGI. Without a watch we'd go mad.

DAR. Or... we could invent time. Cos if I say 'two years later', here, now... then it sort of is two years later.

GIGI. Ha, okay.

DAR (*film trailer voice*). Two years later. Gigi is...?

GIGI. Gigi is... living in the capital.

DAR. Yes, friend!

GIGI. In a penthouse apartment with a view of the ocean.

DAR. Bought by her dad?

GIGI. Paid for by herself!

DAR. How did she pay for such a place?

GIGI. Gigi works... Gigi works as... Gigi writes horoscopes.

DAR (*film trailer voice*). Five years later. Dar lives in Paris. She designs dresses for Dior. Something she does in her spare time, when she's not working for the *UN*. Come meet her gorgeous husband, Nas, he –

GIGI. Thirty years later.

You're living in the eastern suburbs.

DAR. Never!

GIGI. I'm visiting you in your care home. You've got early-onset dementia.

DAR *pretends to have dementia.*

DAR. Fifty years later. You're incontinent.

GIGI *walks like she's shat herself, using her gun as a walking stick.*

GIGI....I've shat myself... Will you wipe me?

DAR....if I remember...

GIGI *laughs.*

A very loud missile flies overhead, startling the audience, but GIGI *and* DAR *don't flinch.*

Before the dude in the go-kart shoots me he takes off his helmet and says, 'Telling this dream to your friend will not stop it from happening it's the usual trick we play with fate but this time it won't work. You will die tomorrow.'

GIGI. It's a dream! Hey show them how quickly you can roll a sleeping bag.

DAR *walks off.*

It's difficult to tell my best friend that her boyfriend had sex with someone else. What makes it harder is… It was me. I had sex with Nas.

It's not how I imagined my first time.

I'm going to tell her. Our friendship is strong enough to handle it.

DAR *enters, unfurls a sleeping bag on the earth.*

DAR. Ready.

GIGI. Go!

DAR *rolls the sleeping bag up at an inhuman speed whilst* GIGI *shouts 'GAS, GAS, GAS, GAS, etc.!'* DAR *finishes.*

You're so good at that, if you could make money rolling sleeping bags you'd be a millionaire – if you had more arms you could roll loads at the same time, you'd be a billionaire – imagine having hundreds of arms, think of what you could do!?! I guess they'd be experimenting on you in a lab, it wouldn't be a life.

DAR *stares at* GIGI.

DAR. Enough, I'm telling you about Nas.

GIGI. Let me enjoy it after duty.

DAR. I'll long it out, do away the time.

GIGI. *Fine.*

DAR. Rearrange your face so it looks happy for me. Friday night – Nas arrives at my house. We'd arranged to have dinner at Wossa, you know Wossa right?

GIGI. I've heard of it.

DAR. So Nas arrives, Mum lets him in, makes a big fuss – quite flirty actually – I'm wearing my white denim shorts and a pink sheer top.

GIGI. What shoes?

DAR. My Gaga monster heels – (GIGI *pulls a face*.) – I like them – so Mum lets him in, Dad gives him a drink, and we all stand around making small talk but Nas keeps giving me this odd look and doing this thing, it's like a spasm, where his arm just goes up.

DAR *demonstrates*.

Like that.

DAR *demonstrates again*.

Weird no?

GIGI. He was nervous.

DAR. Then he says we gotta go, cos we have a reservation at Wossa, so we say bye to my parents and its odd because my dad hugs and kisses him.

GIGI. Nas actually asked for your dad's blessing?

DAR. Yeah.

GIGI. Puke.

DAR. Okay it's puke but it's also really fucking cute, anyways, so we're walking to the restaurant – Nas wants to work up an appetite – I'm starving, I don't need to work up an appetite –

GIGI. Wait did you guess?

DAR. No not at all – so we walk down the street and there's this guy sitting on the sidewalk playing a guitar, and he's got half a leg, like he was born that way, it's not from service. And this guy is singing, and his voice is beautiful and he's singing our song –

GIGI. Are you gonna sing it?

DAR. That's not necessary.

GIGI. Sing – she's got a great voice!

DAR. No no no no, I can't sing.

GIGI. Dar come on –

DAR *sings the first verse of 'Toothpaste Kisses' by The Maccabees brilliantly until –*

DAR. Are you crying?

GIGI. I'm just happy for you.

DAR. Oh sweetie. So I'm singing along with the half-leg guy and I've almost forgotten Nas is there, but then I turn and see him, down on one knee, holding the ring! At first I laugh, like a lot, I even let out a bit of wee which isn't good cos of my tiny shorts, and then we hold each other –

GIGI. What did you have for dinner?

DAR. What?

GIGI. After he proposed didn't you go to that restaurant?

DAR. Wossa was a decoy. Nas had set up a picnic on Thomas Beach. With candles. And fried chicken. It was immense.

GIGI. He should have taken you to Wossa.

DAR. The beach idea was much more romantic.

GIGI. Terrorists once attacked that beach.

DAR. I didn't see any on Friday night.

DAR *takes out an engagement ring from her pocket.*

GIGI. Dar…

DAR *waits for* GIGI *to speak, but she doesn't.*

DAR. Obviously bad stuff went down at that beach, but a place isn't one thing.

GIGI. I guess.

DAR. Par exemple, take this place... one day, it could be a house, a school, a mall.

GIGI. For who?

DAR. For everyone.

GIGI. Everyone?

DAR. I say *everyone*... I'd round up all the extremists and ask them to politely *leave*. Then I'd throw a massive street party. Dress code strictly carnival. Masks, body paint, big hooded capes. Nobody would be recognisable. And by the end of the night, *their* lot are shagging *our* lot.

GIGI. That already happens.

DAR. I'm fantasising about this on an industrial scale.

GIGI. And when the extremists politely refuse to leave?

DAR. Well I'd ask them impolitely.

GIGI. So, you'd kill my dad?

DAR. I'd let your dad live on account of his dimples.

GIGI. Gross.

DAR. Why haven't you looked at my ring?

GIGI *takes the ring. Genuinely admires it.*

GIGI. It's beautiful.

GIGI *returns the ring.*

He doesn't know how lucky he is. You could have anyone.

DAR. What's with the compliments?

GIGI. Just the truth. When you walk into a room, you make an impression.

DAR. So do you.

GIGI. Okay.

DAR. Gigi, whatever you see in me, I see in you.

GIGI. It's cool, you don't need to –

DAR. Shut up – you have an aura.

GIGI. What's an aura?

DAR. It's like a glow, but not like that creepy thing around Jesus's head, the whole of you is shimmering with heat and beauty and light, you landmine of sexiness.

GIGI. Friend, I will take that landmine of sexiness and I will raise it by saying – you are fire you are earth but most of all you are a sass bomb. *A sass bomb.* Come here you bomb of sassiness I gotta handstand incoming.

DAR. INCOMING!

GIGI springs up on her hands, DAR holds her legs and 'walks' her around.

DAR. Yo G. We're special.

GIGI. You sound like my aunt.

DAR. Wait did you ask her about the internship?

GIGI. Oh, I forgot.

DAR. Would you ask?

GIGI. Hey I don't think it pays.

DAR. On the website it says there's assistance.

GIGI. Sure, I'll ask.

Beat.

DAR *drops* GIGI.

Beat.

What's up?

DAR. I can't see it working out. Nothing ever works out.

A huge bomb sound – again GIGI *and* DAR *don't flinch.*

GIGI. You got Nas. That's worked out.

GIGI *looks through her binoculars.*

We have company.

DAR *looks through her binoculars.*

ETA seven minutes.

DAR. Nine.

GIGI. Bet you a boot polish?

DAR. Done.

They put their binoculars down.

GIGI. Dar... Must feel good to know what you're doing after the army.

DAR. Mashed up on shrooms.

GIGI. Beyond that, you know what you'll be. A bride. A mother.

DAR. I'm twenty.

GIGI. Okay not immediately, but eventually you're gonna have kids.

DAR. Friend, what is going on?

GIGI. Absolutely nothing is going on oh my god! It's just cool, you know, to have a life mapped out.

DAR. I swear last month you flipped a coin over being a lawyer or a marine biologist.

GIGI. If Nas asked you to cancel travelling, would you?

DAR. If you don't wanna come, I'll go on my own.

GIGI. I wanna come!

DAR. YEOW it will be the best time we ever have!

GIGI. Yes! Just… sometimes I think all I want is to sit on my couch and wear furry slippers. The quiet of it all. It's not how a nineteen-year-old should be.

DAR. Friend, you'll change your mind when we're dancing in the waves.

GIGI. Yeah.

DAR. Forget this uniform which makes us put on eight pounds. (*Whispered to us*.) We're gonna burn it the day we finish. (*To* GIGI.) Just imagine me in a bikini, you in that orange swimsuit.

GIGI. Huh?

DAR. Orange swimsuit. The all-in-one jobby.

GIGI. I'll be in a bikini.

DAR. Oh, okay.

GIGI. A white one.

DAR. DAMMMMMMN.

GIGI. And I'll be dancing with a guy in one of those moon parties.

DAR. We can dance together, it's not all about the guys.

GIGI. Says you!

DAR. Also, I'm allowed to dance with whoever.

GIGI. I'm sure Nas is cool with that.

DAR. He is, we've had a conversation.

GIGI. You've talked about that?

DAR. We talk about everything.

GIGI. Has he ever cheated on you?

DAR. Never.

GIGI. How do you know?

DAR. Cos he knows I'd castrate him.

GIGI. Harsh.

DAR. You'd let your man get away with cheating?

GIGI. I dunno.

DAR. You'd swallow that?

GIGI. I'd consider the context.

DAR. Fuck the context.

GIGI. What about the girl?

DAR. I'd shoot the girl.

GIGI. Okay so we're going travelling!

DAR. You know I'm all about body positivity, but a white bikini, it's not exactly modest.

GIGI. I could pull it off.

DAR. Yeah yeah yeah you *totally* could. But you shouldn't feel pressure to be anyone but yourself.

GIGI. Are you worried I'll get more attention?

DAR. No I'm not worried.

GIGI. Right.

DAR. No offence.

GIGI. Oh no, none taken.

Although it's not a fair contest is it?

Cos you're likely to be sunbathing topless, and if we're on a beach, we'll be sleeping, or dozing, and when you doze your mouth drops open slightly which gives you a sort of a wanton look, like you look really filthy, and I can imagine that guys might see you and think she looks easy, with her breasts out, and her mouth open, maybe I could just stick my piece in there.

So yes you would get the most attention.

Pause.

DAR. There's this rooftop venue overlooking the ocean. Imagine the ceremony as the sun dips below the waves.

GIGI *turns away*.

I was gonna ask you to be my bridesmaid, but seeing as you clearly don't care –

GIGI. OH MY GOD YES!

DAR. Oh?

GIGI. One hundred percent!

DAR. Yes, friend!

GIGI. What will I wear!?

DAR. We'll choose something together!

OFFICER REMO (*voice-over*). Private Dar, any action? Over.

GIGI *and* DAR *look through their binoculars*.

GIGI. Can't see them now.

DAR. Nothing but sun and dust, over.

The radio stops crackling.

DAR. Let's shoot rubbers!

GIGI. Great! Go get them!

DAR. You're being fucking lazy today.

DAR *exits*.

GIGI. Look how happy she is, she's so happy, I can't tell her. Nas won't tell. His punishment is to carry his guilt to the grave. It will never happen again. I can't tell her. I'm not telling her. Please. Don't judge.

DAR *re-enters*.

DAR. We're out of rubbers.

GIGI. Shit.

DAR. While I was gone did she say anything to you?

Beat.

A phone rings from DAR*'s pocket.*

GIGI. You brought your phone?

DAR. You worried about blue berets now?

GIGI. Always! Don't answer.

DAR. There's nobody here besides us doofuses.

GIGI. A bad message can screw with your head, we've got hours left.

DAR. Calm down it'll be my mum.

GIGI. Doesn't she know your shifts?

DAR. She's going through a bit of a time.

GIGI. Talking to the cat?

DAR. Worse. Tried to put him in the freezer.

A beep.

Mum doesn't leave voicemails. It must be Nas.

GIGI. Don't listen! It's too risky!

DAR. No one's here –

GIGI. If you get caught, you'll be in shit!

DAR. At worst I'll get weekend base duty.

GIGI. Yeah but you're already on a warning – tell them about your warning!

DAR. Last Wednesday I started a food fight.

GIGI. Exactly so you'll get jail!

DAR. Not for picking up my phone.

DAR *takes her phone out of her pocket.*

GIGI *quickly turns and walks away into the scrubland.*

(*Calling out.*) You wanna feel closer to God? Find someone to fall in love with!

DAR *gives the audience a look. Scans the horizon. Listens for patrol cars.*

Listens to the voicemail. We hear a man's voice but we can't make out the words.

GIGI. Was it Nas?

DAR *nods.*

What did he say?

DAR *crouches, winded, stunned at the news she's just received.*

Dar… look. A go-kart.

GIGI *sees the civilians approach.* DAR *follows* GIGI's *eye-line.*

Finally ZOZ *and* SIM *enter the stage, in a small go-kart. It's an epic arrival.*

The car comes to a stop.

DAR *and* GIGI *look at* ZOZ *and* SIM.

GIGI *looks to* DAR *as if she is the one who normally leads.* DAR *remains motionless.*

GIGI. Coming from where?

ZOZ. Section Red.

GIGI. Going to?

ZOZ. BH hospital.

GIGI. What's wrong with your local hospital?

ZOZ. They're overwhelmed with gun-shot wounds.

GIGI. Would you like to speak in your mother tongue?

ZOZ (*to* GIGI). So they don't understand us? (*To audience*.) Are we even in the programme?

SIM. We're not in the title.

GIGI (*in a voice we haven't heard*). You shouldn't be coming this way – it's Section Purple.

ZOZ. Please let us pass and we will quickly get on the road to BH hospital.

GIGI. Turn around, take route twenty-six, exit at roadblock fifty-seven.

SIM. That's forty kilometers away.

GIGI. Calm down young man!

Beat.

ZOZ. Please let me through, I think there is a complication with my baby.

GIGI. [Shit!] Okay, IDs.

ZOZ *hands over their IDs to* GIGI.

Zoz?

ZOZ. Yes.

GIGI. Sim?

SIM *nods*.

Your mother?

SIM *nods*.

DAR. I'll do their passes.

GIGI. Is that necessary?

DAR. Whatever let's not then.

GIGI. No, no, we have too. But quick.

>DAR *walks off towards the cabin.*

>(*Calling out to* DAR *but staring at* SIM.) Bring the book out here.

>Sit.

>ZOZ *and* SIM *sit.*

>*Pause.*

>When are you due?

ZOZ. In two months.

GIGI. Do you know what you're having?

ZOZ. A girl.

>DAR *opens the door of the cabin. Sits on the threshold and opens a ring-binder but doesn't check the passes.*

>Listen.

SIM. Not again.

ZOZ. Come on – last time.

>SIM *sighs and puts his ear to* ZOZ*'s stomach.*

SIM. Sounds like you're hungry.

ZOZ. I'm not hungry. Feel –

SIM. No.

ZOZ. Feel –

SIM. I never feel anything.

ZOZ. Please feel and tell me she's moving.

>SIM *puts his hand on his mother's stomach.*

>*Pause.*

SIM. Yes, something.

ZOZ. Are you sure?

SIM. You always do this. You were like this with Tony.

ZOZ. I haven't felt her move in three days.

SIM. Tony didn't move in nine months, now you can't stop the fucker.

ZOZ. I hate it when you use their curse words.

SIM. Dad does.

ZOZ. Well he's old enough to be a hypocrite.

Pause.

GIGI (*about the car*). Where d'you get this?

Beat.

SIM. I made it.

GIGI. Really?

SIM. Yeah.

Beat.

GIGI. My brother makes cars.

Beat.

SIM. May I ask for who?

GIGI. He works for Hyundai.

SIM. Hyundai. What does he do for them?

ZOZ. Sim!

GIGI. I don't exactly know... but he's part of the design team.

SIM. That's incredible.

ZOZ. Sim be quiet.

GIGI. It's cool.

SIM. Did he design the Hyundai Aslan?

GIGI. I'm not sure.

SIM. What about the Hyundai Stargazer?

GIGI. I don't really know. I sort of zone out when he talks about it.

Beat.

He's very good at it though. Travels to Korea every month. Stays there for a week then travels back.

SIM. Lucky guy!

GIGI. Yes.

Pause.

SIM. What do you drive?

ZOZ. Quiet!

GIGI. It's alright, we're just talking. I don't drive.

SIM. You don't drive?

GIGI. I didn't get around to learning yet.

Beat.

Do you have like a favourite car?

SIM. At the moment it's probably the Datsun Silvia CSP 311. Could I please email your brother?

ZOZ. Sim?!

SIM. Just about cars.

ZOZ. I'm sorry about my son, he's very eager.

SIM. I won't send abuse or anything, I'd just like some careers advice.

Beat.

GIGI. Okay.

ZOZ. Thank you but it's not necessary.

GIGI. It's cool – you got a phone or there's paper / in the cabin.

SIM. I got a phone.

ZOZ. Put that away.

SIM. It's an email address.

ZOZ. You don't need his email –

GIGI. It's fine, you won't get in trouble.

SIM. Mum, please.

ZOZ. No disrespect to your kind offer but I'd rather he didn't.

GIGI. Understood.

Beat.

SIM. Would it be okay to please have a quiet word with my mum?

Beat.

GIGI *walks a little further off.*

You're always telling me to push myself forwards.

ZOZ. At school, not a roadblock.

SIM. She said yes, why would she say yes??

ZOZ. It doesn't need to make sense.

SIM. You can't really stop me.

ZOZ. Yes I can. I can call Fam and tell him to deny you the work experience.

SIM. You wouldn't do that.

ZOZ. Just keep your head down and let's wait quietly.

SIM. Wait quietly!? All we ever do is wait quietly! I'm getting the email.

ZOZ. You don't need their email.

SIM. Yes I do.

ZOZ. You have Fam –

SIM. Fam is a fucking mechanic!

ZOZ. That fucking mechanic might give you a job! It's a future –

SIM. God have mercy, all you and Dad ever talk about is the future, or the past, but never the present. Well guess what, here, in the present, something has turned up!

ZOZ. What could her brother even do for you?

SIM. I dunno! But he might do *something*.

ZOZ *drops her head, resigned.*

SIM. Love you. (*Kisses his mum.*) Excuse me, soldier?

GIGI *walks back over.*

Could I have the email please?

GIGI. Is that okay?

ZOZ. Yes.

GIGI *puts it in* SIM*'s phone.*

GIGI. That's his personal one. I can't remember his Hyundai email, but when I finish shift I'll message him and tell him to expect your email.

SIM. Tell him to check his junk, I'll be emailing from an encrypted account with a fake name.

GIGI. Okay, I mean we have your real name, should there be any / trouble.

SIM. There won't be any trouble.

GIGI. Cool.

SIM. Awesome.

Beat.

GIGI. Let me go check on these passes.

GIGI *sees* DAR *has closed the ring binder.* GIGI *tries to talk to* DAR *but she shrugs her off.* GIGI *picks up the ring binder and starts checking the names.*

SIM. Look at all these people.

ZOZ. Mm.

SIM. Do they know where we are?

ZOZ. Not sure.

SIM. Should we tell them?

ZOZ leans forward and studies them.

ZOZ. No. They might not be on our side.

Beat.

SIM. Do we smile?

ZOZ. Always.

ZOZ smiles at audience.

SIM does the peace sign.

They'll have phones. If anything goes awry, they can be witnesses.

SIM. Those girls aren't gonna do anything.

ZOZ. Says who?

SIM. You can spot the psychos from space.

ZOZ. No you can't, so keep your eyes on the ground.

SIM shakes his head.

Thanks for driving me.

Was Lou disappointed?

SIM. It was only a homework session.

ZOZ. You'll see her again. She likes you.

SIM. Can you not…

ZOZ. Yes, yes, of course. None of my business.

Beat.

Would Lou describe herself as religious?

SIM. Mum.

ZOZ. Just a question.

SIM. Lou doesn't believe in God.

ZOZ. How d'you know?

SIM. She told me.

ZOZ. Right. Well. Lovely girl. And good she doesn't believe in anything. You don't want them too religious.

SIM. I'm gonna write this email.

ZOZ. Now?

SIM. There's literally nothing else to do.

ZOZ. You'll talk to your mum is what you'll do.

SIM. The baby is fine.

ZOZ. I know the baby is fine.

SIM. So I don't need to talk and distract… just… chill.

SIM *starts to write the email.*

ZOZ *steals a glance at the two soldiers on the threshold of the cabin.*

ZOZ. Don't make eye contact with the quiet one. She's upset.

SIM. We've just arrived.

ZOZ. Not about us. Something else.

ZOZ *steals another glance.*

Looks a bit like Lou actually. Don't you think?

SIM. A bit.

ZOZ. Pretty girl – Lou.

SIM. You know Lou and I just do homework.

ZOZ. Yes, yes of course, homework.

SIM. Seriously.

ZOZ. Darling, I'm not interfering –

SIM. Aren't you?

ZOZ. You must study with whoever you / want

SIM. Lou and I are just friends –

ZOZ. The perfect basis for a relationship –

SIM. God have mercy, she's queer!

Beat.

ZOZ. What?

SIM. Forget it.

ZOZ. Lou is gay!?

SIM. We're not talking about this.

ZOZ. Is she just gay? Or does she swing both ways –

SIM. Enough!

ZOZ. Right. Well. You'd never guess. (SIM *pulls a face.*) What? I'm simply saying it isn't apparent.

SIM. Cos she's never come onto you over the supper table?

ZOZ. No! Yes! I'm too old for her.

SIM. MUM!?!

ZOZ. Sorry, sorry. It's just a surprise. Your father and I often talk about you two getting married.

SIM. Please be quiet.

ZOZ. Well, that's the end of that one. Pretty Lou-Lou is gay.

SIM *returns to writing the email.*

If she's gay, why spend so much time at her house?

SIM. Because she's good at maths!

ZOZ. Right yep sorry.

Beat.

SIM. And I like…

ZOZ. Oh.

SIM. Just my luck.

ZOZ. Oh my sweet.

SIM. It's cool.

ZOZ. If I could take away your pain.

SIM. It's okay.

ZOZ. But then you wouldn't be you.

SIM. Yeah all good.

ZOZ. Long term, this rejection will shape you in a positive sense.

SIM. Mum –

ZOZ. Crushes are hard.

SIM. Can you / stop

ZOZ. Crushes are hard but then they pass.

SIM. This isn't a crush!

ZOZ. Oh my darling, oh my love – you've dodged a bullet.

SIM. How?

ZOZ. What do you want with a godless dyke?

SIM. Mum!

ZOZ. That was a joke. (*To the audience.*) I love the gays.

There's no reason why you can't stay friends.

SIM. …Lou will move away soon.

Her heart is set on living with the enemy.

ZOZ. Now I've heard it all.

SIM. They like queers.

ZOZ. Not our queers.

SIM. There's a dude who can get you enemy citizenship for a hundred and seventy-five thousand.

Beat.

ZOZ. Lou would never betray her family like that.

GIGI *walks back and hands IDs to* ZOZ *and* SIM.

DAR *trails behind.*

GIGI. Drive on.

ZOZ. Thank you for helping my son. On my life, he will only send one respectful email.

GIGI. Cool, hope it leads to something.

SIM. Thank you.

DAR. What's all this?

GIGI. He's into cars so I'm connecting him with my bro.

DAR. Sorry, what?

GIGI. What?

DAR. You're connecting him with your brother?

GIGI. Yes.

ZOZ. Sim, drive.

SIM *turns the ignition.*

DAR. Stop!

GIGI. Dar she's pregnant.

DAR. She doesn't look pregnant. Have you looked at their IDs?

GIGI. What?

DAR. ID!?

ZOZ *and* SIM *nonplussed, hand back over their IDs to* DAR.

DAR. Zoz?

ZOZ. ...Yes.

DAR. Sim?

SIM. ...Yes.

DAR. Your mother?

SIM. Yes.

DAR. What is this car? A fucking toy?

SIM. My mum needs to see a doctor.

GIGI. She needs a doctor.

DAR. Do you have proof of ownership for this car?

SIM. It's not exactly an Aston Martin.

DAR. Don't get smart, boy.

GIGI. Okay drive on –

DAR. Private Gigi, I've not finished! Do you have a licence?

SIM. You don't need a licence for a go-kart if you're sixteen and not driving on roads.

DAR. What d'you call this?

SIM. This isn't a road.

DAR. Yes it fucking is – where's your car licence!?

SIM. This is bullshit.

ZOZ. Sim! Soldier, please, our car is in the garage, this is quicker than walking.

DAR. Get out of the car.

GIGI. Private Dar –

DAR. GET OUT OF THE CAR.

ZOZ and SIM get out of the car.

DAR (*to* ZOZ). Lift up you skirt. (*To* SIM.) Open your shirt.

ZOZ *and* SIM *oblige.* DAR *inspects their bodies.*

Sit down there.

ZOZ *and* SIM *sit on the ground.*

GIGI. What are you doing?

DAR. Checking the car.

GIGI. For what?

DAR. Explosives.

GIGI. It's a go-kart!

DAR. Last month a unit found explosives in an ambulance.

GIGI. Where are they going to hide the explosives!?

DAR. Maybe the car is the explosive!

GIGI. Well then *we* shouldn't be searching it!? Radio Officer Remo to bring down the robot!

DAR. We're making our presence felt!

DAR *turns the go-kart upside down and inspects at a painstakingly slow pace. Might empty out contents from a glove box...*

DAR *gestures to* SIM *with her finger to approach.*

Pick up your shit.

SIM *picks up stuff. He talks to the soldiers as he does it.*

SIM. I've recently got into meditation, you ever tried it? A quiet place helps but I can do it anywhere. Last week I meditated in the changing room of my mum's dress shop. Bit of a mad one actually. I thought I was alone, but then I hear my mum come in with a customer. They're talking about a dress fitting. Lucky for me the customer says she's too self-conscious to try it on in the changing room, what with the mirrors, so my mum puts on the closed sign and shuts the blinds. In the middle of the shop, the customer takes off her clothes. And she's big, like oil painting big. And I'm no pervert, but she's quite sexy, so man keeps looking. Mum goes to zip up the dress, and it's like trying to squeeze a rhinoceros into a wetsuit. The customer is holding her breath, Mum is wrestling with the zipper, the zipper is coming out on top, and I think it's all gonna blow. I'm trying so hard not to laugh that I fart. My mum calls out. 'Sim, is that you back there?' I'm like rah... did she recognise the sound, or the smell?

Beat.

DAR. Is something funny?

SIM. No.

DAR. You're smiling.

SIM. I'll stop.

Beat.

DAR. How old are you?

SIM. Sixteen.

DAR. Yo G, doesn't he look like Zayn from One Direction?

GIGI. What?

DAR (*to* SIM). You ever been with a woman?

GIGI. Dar!?

DAR (*to* GIGI). Fancy a go with him? Save you practicing with the fridge?

ZOZ stands up. GIGI approaches ZOZ who stops in her tracks.

A charged pause.

(*To* SIM.) Undress.

SIM. Pardon?

GIGI. Private Dar!?

DAR. Undress.

> SIM *undresses until he is down to his boxers and then* DAR *signals for him to stop.* SIM *looks at his mum, who is looking at the ground, and then looks to the audience.*

Dance.

SIM. Pardon?

DAR. Dance.

> SIM *dances in silence. This goes on for way too long. He looks at his mum whose eyes are on the ground, and then looks to the audience.*

Now sing.

> SIM *wets himself.*

[Ugh…] (*To* GIGI.) He's pissed himself.

> SIM *briefly looks at his mother, who is still looking at the ground.*

Get dressed.

> SIM *puts his clothes back on.*

GIGI. In the car both of you. Go.

> ZOZ *and* SIM *drive off.*
>
> *The car disappears.*

What was that?!

DAR. I was doing my / job.

GIGI. You normally shake their hands.

DAR. I was making our presence / felt.

GIGI. You humiliated him –

DAR. I was taking precautions!

GIGI. Take precautions with terrorists! Not pregnant women and boys in toy fucking cars!

DAR. Nas went with someone.

GIGI. What?

DAR. Nas went with someone at the Block.

GIGI. Did he say who?

DAR. It doesn't make sense, he isn't, he isn't one of those guys, oh god, maybe –

GIGI. So you don't know who?

DAR. Some cunt. Hey you were there – did you see anything?

GIGI. No.

DAR. You went to the Block with Tina.

GIGI. Yeah, so –

DAR. Call her and find out if she saw anything.

GIGI. Okay.

DAR. Now.

GIGI. I'll do it after duty.

DAR. Do it now.

GIGI. I'll do it straight after duty, promise.

DAR. Do it now –

GIGI. What else did he say on the voicemail?

DAR. That he loves me and wants to spend the rest of his life with me.

GIGI. Coward.

DAR. Why coward?

GIGI. If he wants to spend the rest of his life with you, he should have had the courage to swallow what he'd done and not told you.

DAR. Why shouldn't he have told me?

GIGI. Because you'd never have known.

DAR. Then I would have been living a lie.

GIGI. But you wouldn't. He still loves you, and you'd never have known.

DAR. I'd have found out.

GIGI. How!?

DAR. I'm a DJ – I know everyone who is hooking up!

GIGI. So now you know, what you gonna do?

DAR. If you saw something you'd tell me right.

GIGI. I didn't see anything.

DAR. I know, it's just, what you said before makes me think you wouldn't tell me.

GIGI. I didn't see anything.

DAR. But you'd tell me wouldn't you? Cos if the situation was reversed and I saw something – I won't be angry, it's not like it's your responsibility to stop him.

GIGI. I need the toilet.

GIGI *disappears around the back of the cabin.*

DAR. She saw something. The girl can't lie.

GIGI *re-emerges from the cabin with two IV bags.*

GIGI. Got some IV... thought you could do with it.

DAR. Check you breaking the rules.

GIGI. Yeah...

They roll up their sleeves and stick the needles in their veins.

Pause.

DAR. Was it Tina?

GIGI. Huh?

DAR. Did Tina go with Nas?

GIGI. No.

DAR. Swear on my life.

GIGI. I swear on your life.

DAR. To what?

GIGI. I swear on your life that Tina did not sleep with Nas.

Pause.

DAR. You waxed your monobrow?

GIGI. Yeah.

DAR. Looks good.

GIGI. Thanks.

DAR. Tina is quite hairy.

GIGI. Her grandparents came from the south.

DAR. D'you think she looks like a Yeti?

GIGI. I don't know what that is.

DAR. Whatever, she's hot. Her face is devastating.

GIGI. Girl crush?

DAR. Nas told me he kissed a girl at the Block. He didn't say anything about sleeping with one.

Why do you think Nas has slept with somebody?

GIGI. I don't. I just assumed by what you... if he said he just kissed you should take his word for it.

DAR *looks down at her veins.*

DAR. That was shit of me... what I did to the boy.

Didn't even know I was capable of that.

GIGI. Whatever... just don't do it again.

DAR *takes out her phone.*

GIGI. Who are you calling?

DAR. Nas.

> GIGI *rips the needle out of her vein, snatches the phone and hangs up.* DAR *rips the needle out of her vein.*

GIGI!?

GIGI. Let's talk this out before you / call.

DAR (*reaching for the phone*). I need to know how it went / down.

> GIGI *pulls away.*

WHAT THE ACTUAL FUCK?

The radio crackles.

OFFICER REMO (*voice-over*). Private Dar, we picked up a boy and his mother. She was bleeding. We've driven them to BH hospital. Did you see them? Over.

Beat.

Private Gigi did you see the boy and mother over?

DAR. Nothing our way they must have exited at checkpoint 57 over.

Give me the phone!

GIGI. The pregnant woman is bleeding!?!

DAR. Give me the phone!

GIGI. I had sex with Nas.

Beat.

DAR. Don't mess with me like that. It was Tina.

GIGI. It was me.

DAR....?

GIGI. It didn't mean anything.

DAR. Gigi...

GIGI. I love you.

DAR. No – shut up – no.

GIGI. Dar, I'm so –

DAR. No no no no no no no.

   DAR *backs away.*

   GIGI *follows.*

GIGI. Dar please –

DAR. Come any closer I'll shoot.

   DAR *sits herself down on a rock far away.*

   DAR *lights a cigarette.*

GIGI. Please Dar, you'll get into so much shit.

   DAR *smokes.*

Some time.

What's the time?

182?

   GIGI *picks up a rock. Takes out a marker pen. Starts to colour it.*

Look, it's a baby. (*Puppeteering the rock.*)

Wah. Wah. Waaaaaaaah. Stupid baby. Stupid fucking baby.

   GIGI *tosses the rock, killing the 'baby'.*

Some time.

125?

DAR *checks her watch but doesn't respond.*

GIGI *checks the coast is clear. Applies eyeliner.*

Eighty-four?

GIGI *wipes off her eye-liner.*

Seventy-three?

DAR. The worst thing about this… is that when something bad happens to me, I talk to you. Now who do I talk to?

SIM *enters, his face blotchy like he's been crying.*

Time slows down.

DAR *sees* SIM *approach* GIGI. GIGI *is still colouring rocks, oblivious.* SIM *raises up a large medical scalpel.* DAR *watches* SIM *stab* GIGI*'s neck.* SIM *lifts his hand for a second stab but* DAR *shoots him. Time speeds up. A sustained volley of shots drives* SIM *backwards. He collapses. A huge dust cloud rises to the sky.*

GIGI!

GIGI. See to the boy!

The radio crackles.

OFFICER REMO (*voice-over*). Private Dar we heard shots. Over.

GIGI. Officer Remo, we've been –

DAR. Officer Remo, just practice. Over.

OFFICER REMO (*voice-over*). Were shots fired? Over.

GIGI. Yes –

DAR. JUST TARGET PRACTICE! Over.

GIGI. DAR!?!

OFFICER REMO (*voice-over*). Use rubber next time. Over.

DAR. Affirmative. Over.

GIGI. Radio back.

DAR. No.

GIGI. What?!

DAR. You're going to be okay!

GIGI. For the boy!

DAR. I should have shot him in the leg!

SIM. You should have!

GIGI. Radio Officer Remo, for an ambulance!

DAR. We can't, I'll be in trouble.

GIGI. RADIO OFFICER REMO!

DAR. Shut the fuck up SHUT THE FUCK UP!

SIM. I don't normally get sick... I chew bread and spit it in the toilet to get days off from school... Dad falls for it... not Mum... always sends me in... am I hurt badly?

DAR *shakes her head*.

Phew.

DAR *tries to smile at* SIM.

I thought she was you.

DAR....

SIM. I didn't want to hurt *her.*

DAR. She'll be okay.

SIM. Good.

You look like my friend Lou.

DAR. People always say I look like other people.

SIM. Lou prefers women.

DAR. Oh.

SIM. I'm completely in love with her.

DAR....

SIM. Come closer.

DAR *comes closer.*

(*Softly.*) My brothers are young... but they will find you, and kill you, and kill your parents and kill your future children and we will burn your houses, and burn your people, and when you are ash, from the ash we will plant, we will build and – look in my eyes so you don't forget me. We are not going anywhere. You can change the road signs, flatten our homes, stamp out our language, but we will build, and we will plant and we will... I wanted to work in Japan... Shit...! Tell my dad I didn't cry... tell him I wasn't scared... tell him I cursed you until –

SIM *dies.*

Pause.

GIGI. Radio Remo.

DAR. We weren't straight.

GIGI. Radio Remo –

DAR. Why is he here?

GIGI. Stop –

DAR. This is our show – he isn't dead – he isn't here!? Yo, get up! Wake up!

GIGI. DAR STOP! Where's his mum?

DAR. Fuck!

GIGI. Radio Remo. When it comes to real things Remo knows what / to do.

DAR. I've killed a boy.

GIGI. He had a / blade.

DAR. I've killed a boy.

GIGI. It was self-defence.

DAR. Yes. Where's the blade?

GIGI. Yeah the blade.

DAR. He had a blade! They saw a blade!

The audience saw a blade because there was one, and yet... after much scrabbling in the earth, all DAR *can find is a toy screwdriver.*

GIGI. That's a toy!

DAR. There was a blade! I saw a massive fucking –

GIGI. RADIO REMO!

DAR. There'll be questions, a tribunal.

GIGI. What are you saying...?

DAR. Why didn't you tell me about Nas before shift?

GIGI. Dar shut up!

DAR. I would have had time to process –

GIGI. Stop! There's a dead boy –

DAR. If you'd told me earlier, I could have swallowed it –

GIGI. Are you actually trying to justify your / reaction!?

DAR. Why didn't you tell me!?

GIGI. I didn't know how! I told them!

GIGI *gives a look to the audience.*

DAR *spins to look at the audience.*

The radios crackle.

OFFICER REMO (*voice-over*). Private Dar anything? Over.

Beat.

Private Gigi any action? Over.

DAR. No action but sun and dust. Over.

GIGI *investigates* SIM.

GIGI. He should be at home, he should be studying, he should be listening to music, he should be at the beach, he should be in a café, he should be shopping, he should be with his mum.

DAR. Stop with the poetry. Sixty-two minutes. We bury the boy. Back at base, we say you tripped and cut your neck.

GIGI. You wanna cover this up?

DAR. There was no weapon.

GIGI. So?

DAR. It'll go on my record, affect jobs, my parents will be so –

GIGI. If anything you'll be commended – you killed to protect me –

DAR. I'm not a killer... I can plait hair... I'm on the left...

GIGI. You've done nothing wrong.

DAR. We're burying the boy!

GIGI. We don't need too.

DAR. He must disappear.

GIGI. Disappear!?

DAR. Was the boy holding a toy or a blade!?

GIGI. It doesn't matter, he's dead.

DAR. The facts won't stay still!

GIGI. Just calm down.

DAR. Calm down!? The girl who sleeps through missiles, yet wakes up screaming if you whisper in her ear, is telling me to calm down. We're burying the boy.

GIGI. I won't do it.

DAR: Yes you will.

Pause.

(*Hopeful.*) I think he must be with his mum now.

GIGI....yeah.

DAR. We should take comfort in that.

GIGI. Yes.

***

The earth is flat again. As if SIM *was never there.*

Some time.

DAR. How could you do it with Nas?

GIGI *is horrified by the question. As is* DAR.

Pause.

GIGI. I wanted to do it. Everyone does it before they finish the army. And so I went to the Block, and wore almost nothing, I looked like you.

DAR. What the fuck Gigi? Why?

GIGI. I went over to Nas. I offered him drinks. He said no at first. But I pushed. We did shots. And then I whispered in his ear. And we walked into the toilets.

It lasted a few minutes. The moment after he came, he cried.

DAR. What are you telling me this for?

GIGI. So you know it all.

Beat.

DAR. You've fucked us Gigi.

GIGI.... You've fucked us more my love

GIGI looks down at the spot where they buried SIM.

DAR looks down at the spot.

DAR's watch goes beep.

DAR. Five more days. Five more days. And then no more white cheese, no more burnt toast, no more tying our hair up ever again, we're gonna travel the world, get high –

GIGI. We're gonna be here longer than five days.

DAR (*cheery*). Do you remember your draft day? I'd not slept! My tonsils were the size of figs. The doctor said I'd have be drafted the following week. I started to cry... I was so desperate to start... the doctor said you'll soon be crying to go home. I thought it would be like camp. With guns. But still camp.

GIGI. Dar we're going to have to lie for forever.

A moment.

From the barren earth, flowers begin to bloom. It becomes a carpet of anemones, cyclamen, blue iris, pink flax, Maltese cross and pyramid orchids. We can smell blue sage and thyme. It is all very overpowering.

GIGI and DAR stare at each other, totally baffled at the sudden change of season.

ZOZ enters pushing an old-fashioned pram. The walking boots and the rucksack suggest she's been walking for some time.

GIGI. You had the baby?

ZOZ. I did.

GIGI *smiles. And then she remembers.*

Pause.

DAR. Coming from?

ZOZ. Home.

DAR. Going to?

ZOZ. Here.

DAR. Here!? Here's isn't a place. It's a roadblock.

ZOZ. Why is it a roadblock, something must have happened?

DAR. Nothing happened. Look if you want to carry on, exit at checkpoint 57.

ZOZ. I want to explore here.

DAR. Explore!? Be my guest, yeah, tap dance while you're at it!? Fucking sing for all I care!

ZOZ surprises everyone including herself by starting to sing.

Okay stop.

Beat.

GIGI. You've got a lovely voice.

ZOZ. Took losing a son to find it.

He ran off from the hospital... he thought I'd lost the baby. I shouted for him to come back but he was in a rage. You know when people get like that, they can't hear a thing. Have you seen him?

DAR. Not since earlier. With you.

ZOZ. That was months ago.

GIGI and DAR exchange a look.

I've spoken to the police, and an NGO who helps with missing persons, but there's nothing. There is no trace of him. It's like my son vanished off the face of the earth. The police tell me the case is still open but I see how they look at me.

As if I'm too stupid to accept the inevitable. What about you – did you see him?

GIGI. No.

ZOZ. Maybe he came back and you forgot.

DAR. He hasn't come back this way.

ZOZ. Would it help if I described him?

DAR. We remember what he looks like – where's the relief car?

GIGI. The car is always a bit late.

ZOZ. It'll be no surprise to you that my son loves cars. His teachers tell me he spends all of lessons drawing cars. I don't understand where the passion comes from. I have a dress shop. His father is a drugs counsellor – we have no interest in machines. Perhaps that explains his passion. As a child he wanted to be the man who makes the gadgets for James Bond. So we arranged an apprenticeship with a mechanic. My son obviously missed it last summer, but the offer is still open. For when he returns.

Beat.

GIGI. Would you like some Nutella?

ZOZ. ...Why not.

DAR. We don't have a spoon.

ZOZ. I do.

ZOZ produces a baby spoon and starts eating the Nutella.

GIGI. It's dangerous to be walking around these parts with a baby.

ZOZ. Even you wouldn't hurt a mother and a baby would you?

DAR. So she's a pawn for your protection?

ZOZ. Yes. No. I can't deny her spring.

DAR. I'd like to go back to base now.

GIGI. The car is coming!

ZOZ. When you forced Sim to dance, I kept my eyes on the ground. That moment haunts me. If I'd looked at him I would have been able to make it okay. I'd have been able to say with my eyes, that whatever these soldiers are trying to make you feel, you don't need to feel it. I could have reframed the moment into something more bearable.

ZOZ returns to eating the Nutella and staring at DAR.

DAR (into radio). Private Dar and Private Gigi awaiting relief car. Over.

Beat.

(*Into radio.*) Officer Remo, permission to be relieved. Over.

Beat.

(*Into radio.*) Officer Remo, there is no car or Private Viv or Private Kaz. Over!

ZOZ. Maybe your army has moved onto a new front.

DAR. Our army doesn't leave soldiers behind.

ZOZ. Where are they then?

DAR looks around.

Have they been abandoned?

DAR (*in a low voice*). Let's go.

GIGI. Where?

DAR. Back to base.

GIGI. Don't be an idiot.

DAR. Our shift is over!

GIGI. We stay until we're relieved!

DAR. Fuck that. Come on.

GIGI. I'm staying.

DAR. Gigi!?

GIGI. Get in line.

DAR. I forgive you I forgive you.

GIGI. Private Dar get in line!

DAR. You cannot stay if I leave.

GIGI. Nobody is leaving.

DAR. I can't breathe.

GIGI. Yes you can.

DAR. She's looking at me.

GIGI. Keep it together.

DAR. I can't –

DAR drops her head slightly.

GIGI. Stand tall.

DAR. I can't –

GIGI. Stand fucking tall.

DAR. Gigi please!

GIGI. I will report you to Commander Quin if you don't stand fucking tall!

DAR unclips her gun.

Fucksake!?!

GIGI picks up DAR's gun. Clips it back onto DAR's belt.

DAR. [I hate this I hate this I hate this I want the ground to swallow me up.]

Pause.

GIGI. Should we tell her?

Beat.

DAR. I just want to go home, G.

GIGI doesn't budge.

DAR. Please…

GIGI moves away.

DAR looks at her friend, completely bewildered.

Exits the stage.

GIGI quietly gasps.

ZOZ. Brave girl to run off in these parts.

GIGI. She's got a gun.

ZOZ. Who's fazed by a lone soldier with a gun.

Beat.

What upsets your friend?

GIGI. Just personal stuff.

Beat.

ZOZ. There is the possibility that Sim went to live with your people. That he got citizenship, and he lives now in your capital, and okay he's changed his name and okay he has a job that pays taxes to your army but when I imagine him sat in a café with a friend… I feel only joy. His father and I couldn't give him the life he deserved so he ran. Now, perhaps my boy, for shame, hasn't made contact. And I think you, with who your father is, may have special access to information, and if you could just tell me if my boy is living… and to pass on a message that his mother loves him and is proud of him for pursuing his passion, no matter what.

GIGI. Can I see your baby?

ZOZ flinches.

ZOZ. You don't believe I have a baby?

GIGI. I do I'm just curious.

ZOZ. About what?

GIGI. I like babies. I'd never hurt one.

Beat.

ZOZ. She's sleeping.

GIGI. I won't make a sound.

GIGI unclips her gun and lays it down.

ZOZ steps away.

GIGI looks in on her baby.

GIGI. She's... She's so...

ZOZ. Ugly, I know. They all look like their father at this stage, and then as they grow up, they start to look more like me.

GIGI. She's so big. Isn't she a few hours old?

ZOZ. Oh no, you're all over the place. She's eight months.

GIGI. What?

ZOZ. She is eight months old.

GIGI. That's... that's not possible...!?

ZOZ. I know when my baby was born. Or do you people now control time?

Beat.

GIGI turns back to the baby.

ZOZ walks towards the gun.

GIGI. Huh, she's pouting...

ZOZ is next to the gun. Looks at us.

What's her name?

ZOZ. Oh I won't name her until she's about five.

GIGI. Why?

ZOZ. Less painful, if anything were to happen. Once you name them, you get attached.

Beat.

GIGI. I'm gonna get my eggs frozen.

ZOZ. Aren't you a bit young to think like that?

ZOZ hands hover over the gun.

GIGI. Takes the pressure off finding someone. And this way I can have a platoon of babies.

GIGI turns around and sees that ZOZ is near the gun.

ZOZ. A platoon of babies? What's next – 'your womb is your weapon'? You stupid girl, you stupid little girl. Have one baby. Love one baby. And then lose him! I've thought about this moment, I've dreamt of your death, worse – your evaporation, your mother left in a daze, driven insane by questions with no answers!! If my son is dead how can it rain? If my son is dead why is everything growing? Why is nature not in revolt!

ZOZ starts to dig in the earth.

I must find my son, I must quiet this feeling, I can't mother my other children with this feeling!?

GIGI. Your son is here.

GIGI points to the place he was buried.

ZOZ digs in the earth and finds her son.

ZOZ. Hello my darling.

Some time.

GIGI. Let me speak to my officer about how we, what the process is for delivering your son back to… I guess you want him buried in your town.

Beat.

ZOZ. Yes. And then what?

GIGI sits back.

Snap to black.

A Nick Hern Book

Gigi & Dar first published in Great Britain as a paperback original in 2024 by Nick Hern Books Limited, The Glasshouse, 49a Goldhawk Road, London W12 8QP

Gigi & Dar copyright © 2024 Josh Azouz

Josh Azouz has asserted his right to be identified as the author of this work

Cover design by Madison Coby

Designed and typeset by Nick Hern Books, London
Printed in Great Britain by Mimeo Ltd, Huntingdon, Cambridgeshire PE29 6XX

A CIP catalogue record for this book is available from the British Library

ISBN 978-1-83904-402-1

CAUTION All rights whatsoever in this play are strictly reserved. Requests to reproduce the text in whole or in part should be addressed to the publisher.

Amateur Performing Rights Applications for performance, including readings and excerpts, by amateurs in the English language should be addressed to the Performing Rights Manager, Nick Hern Books, The Glasshouse, 49a Goldhawk Road, London W12 8QP, *tel* +44 (0.)20 8749 4953, *email* rights@nickhernbooks.co.uk, except as follows.

Australia: ORiGiN Theatrical, *tel* +61 (2.) 8514 5201, *email* enquiries@originmusic.com.au, *web* www.origintheatrical.com.au

New Zealand: Play Bureau, 20 Rua Street, Mangapapa, Gisborne 4010, *tel* +64 21 258 3998, *email* info@playbureau.com

Professional Performing Rights Applications for performance by professionals in any medium and in any language throughout the world should be addressed to Independent Talent Group Ltd, 40 Whitfield Street, London W1T 2RH, *tel* +44 (0)20 7636 6565

No performance of any kind may be given unless a licence has been obtained. Applications should be made before rehearsals begin. Publication of this play does not necessarily indicate its availability for amateur performance.

www.nickhernbooks.co.uk/environmental-policy

www.nickhernbooks.co.uk

facebook.com/nickhernbooks
twitter.com/nickhernbooks